R.I.P.

you'll never get out
of it alive, so pick your
favorite!

2/21/70

THE LAST LAUGH

*A Completely
New Collection of
Funny Old Epitaphs
Disinterred by
Gail Peterson
Revitalized with
Likenesses by
John Trotta*

HALLMARK EDITIONS

About THE LAST

LAUGH

We expect epitaphs to be serious
memorials. Most tombstone in-
scriptions today and in the past
meet our expectations. But our
recent ancestors didn't worry as
we do about seriousness. Some-
times by accident, usually delib-
erately, they inscribed humorous
verses over the graves of their departed.

Perhaps they were warming
with their humor the chill of the
unknown. More obviously, they
devoutly believed that death is
only a doorway to an afterlife, a
dark shadow that deserves a last
laugh. "Death, be not proud,"
John Donne wrote in his famous

sonnet, "though some have called thee/Mighty and dreadful, for thou art not so. . . ." And thus, unlikely as it seems, we find humor in graveyards. Nothing could be more human, for only men can laugh.

Many old books record the unusual verses carved on gravestones in antique cemeteries in England and America. Most of the epitaphs in this book are authentic; a few are questionable, but have been included here because they are traditional and amusing. Consider them all in good spirit: the deceased they memorialize do.

Reader, pass on!

CRYPTIC WIT

On a healthy man's life:

Here lies the body of

Samuel Procter,

Who lived and died without

a doctor.

*A questionable tribute to a man
frozen to death in wintertime:*

The winter snow

congealed his form

But now we know

our Uncle's warm.

Here lies the body of John Smith

Buried in the cloisters;

If he don't jump at the last trump,

Call, "Oysters!"

CHILDWALD, ENGLAND

Here lies Captain John Konkapot.

God, be as good to him as he

would be

If he were God and You were

John Konkapot.

STOCKBRIDGE CENTER, MASS.

*W*hile on earth

my knee was lame,

I had to nurse

and heed it.

But now

I'm at a better place

Where I don't

even need it.

ITHACA, NEW YORK

8

Fame carries far, this gravestone implies:

Here lies two grandsons of

John Hancock, first signer of the

Declaration of Independence.

(Their names are respectively

Geo. M. and John H. Hancock)

and their eminence hangs on

their having had a grandfather.

Sacred to the memory

of three twins.

Molly, tho' pleasant in her day,

Was sudd'nly seized and sent away.

How soon she's ripe,

how soon she's rotten,

Laid in the grave and soon

forgotten.

MILFORD, CONN.

A traveller lies here at rest

Who life's rough ocean tossed on.

His many virtues all expressed

Thus simply—"*I'm from Boston.*"

ST. BOTOLPH'S, ENGLAND

Drink never hurt this good lady:

She drank good ale,

good punch, and wine,

And liv'd to the age

of ninety-nine.

Above cremated remains
appears this inscription:

And this is all that's left of thee

Thou fairest of earth's daughters.

Only four pounds of ashes white

Out of two hundred and three

quarters.

A widow tries her best:

Here lies the remains of

Thomas Woodhen,

The most amiable of husbands,

and excellent of men.

N. B. His real name was

Woodcock, but

it wouldn't come in rhyme.

His Widow.

This is what I expected but

not so soon.

WESTERNVILLE, N.Y., 1872

*A*gainst his will
Here lies George Hill
Who from a cliff
Fell down quite stiff;
When it happened
is not known,
Therefore not mention'd
on this stone.

ISLE OF THANET

14

Elizabeth Scott lies buried here.

She was born Nov 20th 1785,

according to the best of her

recollection.

Here lies one Wood

enclosed in wood,

One wood within another.

The outer wood is very good,

We cannot praise the other.

Emery, a coarse stone used for grinding metal, inspired this epitaph:

Ashes to ashes dust to dust,

Here lies George Emery I trust.

And when the trump blows louder

and louder

He'll rise a box of Emery powder.

Here lies Bernard Lightfoot who

was accidentally killed in the

forty fifth year of his age.

Erected by his grateful family.

ST. BOTOLPH'S, ENGLAND

Beneath these stones

repose the bones

Of Theodosius Grimm,

He took his beer from year to year,

And then his bier took him.

DURHAM, ENGLAND

Born 15 September 1822

Accidentally shot

4th April 1844

As a mark of affection

from his brother.

Poor Martha Shiell has gone away,

Her would if she could,

but her couldn't stay;

Her had 2 bad legs

and a baddish cough,

It was her two bad legs

that carried her off.

NEAR LONDON, ENGLAND

Comedian W. C. Fields wanted
this epitaph to appear over his grave:

I'd rather be here than in

Philadelphia.

The famous, cryptic epitaph to
William Shakespeare:

Good frend for Iesvs sake forbeare,

To digg the dvst encloased heare!

Bleste be ye man yt spares

thes stones,

And curst be he yt moves

my bones.

He Called Bill Smith A Liar.

CRIPPLE CREEK, COLORADO

TILL DEATH DID
THEM PART

Sacred to the memory

of Anthony Drake,

Who died for peace

and quietness sake.

His wife was constantly

scolding and scoffing,

So he sought repose

in a twelve dollar coffin.

FALKIRK, ENGLAND

Here lies the body of

Obadiah Wilkinson

And Ruth, his wife.

Their warfare is accomplished.

NEW HAVEN, CONN.

Here lies Jane Smith, wife of
Thomas Smith, marble cutter. This
monument was erected by her husband as a tribute to her memory and
a speciment of his work. Monu-
ments of the same style 350 dollars.

Grieve not for me my Harriet dear

For I am better off.

You know what were

my sufferings

And what a dreadful cough.

GREENWOOD, N.Y.

Farewell dear wife my life is past,

I loved you whilst my life did last.

Weep not for me nor sorrow take,

But love my brother for my sake.

SARATOGA, NEW YORK

Four graves in New London County, Conn.,
carry the following notes
beneath the names of the deceased:

My I wife.

My II wife.

My III wife.

My IIII wife.

In the center of these four
is a grave marked:

Our husband.

Is a husband complaining, or did the
stonecarver leave off the final "e"?

Lord, she is Thin

Here lies Donald & his wife

Janet MacFee

Aged 40 hee

And 30 shee.

A wife's last word:

Stranger, call this not a place of

fear and gloom

To me it is a pleasant spot—

it is my husband's tomb.

Those *that* knew him best

deplored him most.

Sacred to the Memory of

Mr. Jared Bates

who Died Aug. the 6th 1800.

His widow aged 24

who mourns as one

who can be comforted

lived at 7 Elm street

this village

and possesses

every qualification

for a good wife.

LINCOLN, MAINE

Here lies the man Richard,

And Mary his wife;

Their surname was Pritchard,

They lived without strife;

And the reason was plain—

They abounded in riches,

They no care had, nor pain,

And the *wife wore the breeches*.

ESSEX, ENGLAND

This husband's opinion is uncertain:

She was more to me than

I expected.

30

My vife Susum is dead; If she'd had
life till next Friday she'd been dead
shust two weeks. As a tree falls so
must she stand. All things is im-
possible mit God.

Epitaph to an unhappy marriage:

Within this grave do lie

Back to back my wife and I.

When the last trump

the air shall fill,

If she gets up I'll just lie still.

He first departed—she a little tried

To live without him—liked it not and died.

QUORNDON, ENGLAND

Here lies the wife of brother Thomas

Who tyrant death has torn from us,

Her husband never shed a tear,

Until his wife was buried here.

And then he made a fearful rout,

For fear she might find her way out.

VERMONT

This husband cherished the last word:

Here lies wife second of old

Wing Rogers

She's safe from care and I from

bothers!

If death had known thee

as well as I,

He ne'er had stopped

but passed thee by.

I wish him joy, but much I fear

He'll rue the day he came thee near.

*T*his stone

was raised by Sarah's lord,

Not Sarah's virtues

to record, —

For they're well-known

to all the town, —

But it was *raised*

to keep *her down.*

To free me from domestic strife,

Death called at my house, but he

Spoke with my wife.

Susan, wife of David Patterson,

lies here,

Oct. 19, 1706.

Stop reader, and if not in a hurry

shed a tear.

SUFFOLK, ENGLAND

OUT OF BUSINESS

For a clerk, a careful list:

Here lies buried beneath

these stones,

The beard, the flesh,

and all the bones

Of the Parish Clerk—old

David Jones.

Here lies the remains of

JOHN HALL grocer.

The world is not worth a fig

I have good *raisins* for saying so.

John Adams lies here,

of the parish of Southwell,

A carrier who carried his

can to his mouth well;

He carried so much,

and he carried so fast,

He could carry no more,

so was carried at last;

For the liquor he drunk,

being too much for one,

He could not carry off—

so he's now *carri-on!*

In All Saint's Churchyard,
Newcastle England:

Here lies Robert Wallace,

Clerk of All Hallows,

King of good fellows,

And maker of bellows.

He bellows did make

till the day of his death,

But he that made bellows

could never make breath.

Here lies John White,

who day by day

On river works did use much clay,

Is now himself turning that way.

If not to clay, yet dust will come,

Which to preserve takes

little room,

Although inclosed in this

great tomb.

ENFIELD, ENGLAND

Epitaph for a dentist:

View this gravestone

with gravity

He is filling his last cavity.

Here lies the body of poor

Frank Row,

Parish clerk, and grave stone cutter.

And this is writ to let you know,

What Frank for others us'd to do,

Is now for Frank done by another.

YORKSHIRE, ENGLAND

Underneath this crust

Lies the moulding dust

Of Elenor Bachelor Shoven

Well versed in the arts

Of pies, custards and tarts

And the lucrative trade of the oven

When she lived long enough

She made her last puff.

On a gardener's grave:

Transplanted

EASTPORT, MAINE

*On the remains of Robert Trollop,
architect of the Exchange and Town Hall
of Newcastle, England:*

Here lies Robert Trollop,

Who made yon stones roll up.

When death took his soul up,

His body filled this hole up.

On a careless cowboy:

Here lies a man

whose crown was won

By blowing in

an empty gun.

The body of

BENJAMIN FRANKLIN Printer,

Like the Covering of an old Book

Its contents torn out

And stript of its Lettering

and Gilding Lies here,

Food for Worms;

But the Work shall not be lost,

It will (as he believed)

appear once more, In a new

and more beautiful Edition,

Corrected and amended

By the Author.

Benjamin Franklin's own epitaph

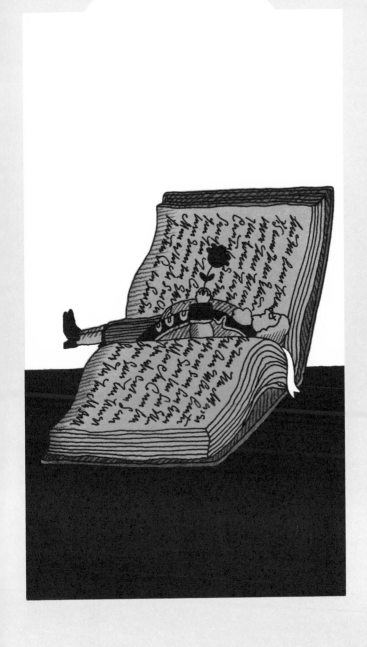

A baker retires:

Throughout his life

he kneaded bread

And deemed it quite a bore.

But now six feet beneath

earth's crust

He needeth bread no more.

A tribute to a fisherman:

He's done a-catching cod

And gone to meet his God.

BLOCK ISLAND, N.Y.

Epitaph for a butcher named Lamb:

Beneath this stone

lies Lamb asleep,

Who died a Lamb

who lived a sheep.

Many a lamb

and sheep he slaughtered

But cruel Death

the scene has altered.

Written for a blind wood sawyer:

While none ever saw him see

thousands have seen him saw.

God works a wonder

now and then,

He, though a lawyer,

was an honest man.

NEW HAVEN, CONN.

On a locksmith:

A zealous locksmith died of late,

And did not enter Heaven's gate.

But stood without

and would not knock

Because he meant to pick the lock.

NEXT TO LAST

JUDGMENTS

Here lies Ned Hyde

because he died.

If it had been his sister

We should not have missed her.

But would rather it had

been his father

Or for the good of the nation

The whole generation.

The Lord don't make any mistakes.

SOUTH PLYMOUTH, N.Y.

Ebenezer Dockwood,

aged forty-seven,

A miser and a hypocrite,

never went to heaven.

MASSACHUSETTS

Here lies the body of

Nancy H. Gwyn,

Who was so very pure within

She burst her outer shell of sin

And hatched herself a cherubin.

NEAR LONDON, ENGLAND

53

The grave for Sheil, an Irish orator,
bears this epitaph:

*H*ere lies I.

There's an end to my woes,

And my spirit

at length at ease is,

With the tip of my nose,

And the

End of my toes,

Turned up against the roots

of the daisies.

Emma, dau'r of Abraham

and Matilda

C———, and wife of

Theodore S———,

died Aug. 10, 1868, Æ 26 yrs.,

leaving five children

—married too young

against her father's will.

Single women take warning.

SARATOGA, N.Y.

56

At rest beneath this slab of stone,

Lies stingy Jimmy Wyett.

He died one morning just at ten

And saved a dinner by it.

FALKIRK, ENGLAND

Just desserts:

Here Doctor Fisher lies interr'd

Who filled the half of this

churchyard.

God takes the good too good on

earth to stay,

God leaves the bad too bad to

take away.

NEW YORK, N.Y.

Here lies the body of

Dr. Hayward,

A man who never voted.

Of such is the kingdom of

Heaven.

WAYLAND, MASS.

A hard testimonial marks this man's grave:

Here lies a man who did no good,

And if he'd lived he never would;

Where he's gone or how he fares,

Nobody knows and nobody cares.

Here lies John Hill

A man of skill,

His age was five time ten,

He ne'er did good

Nor ever would

Had he lived as long again.

MANCHESTER, ENGLAND

A youth of real worth

lies buried here,

Who had but just attained

his 17th year,

Yet in that time such wisdom

had he shown,

That death mistook 17 for 71.

SUFFOLK, ENGLAND

Now Aint

That Too Bad

CHICAGO, ILL., 1907

Reader, pass on!

—don't waste your time

On bad biography

and bitter rhyme;

For what I *am*,

this crumbling clay insures,

And what I *was*,

is no affair of yours!

NEW JERSEY

Set in Janson-Antiqua
a typeface born
in the 17th Century Baroque
but timeless
because of its clarity and legibility,
its Creation ascribed to
Anton Janson (1620-1687).
Preserved upon
Hallmark Eggshell Book paper
and Designed by Harald Peter
Who, As of this Printing,
Is Alive and Well.